I'm Happy!

by Ashley Blackburn

Health

Content Vocabulary

book

car

computer

drink

granddad

park

phone

shoulder

snow tube

swimming

I'm happy when
I'm in the park,
and I'm happy when
I wash the car.

washing the car

We are in the park
with our mother.

I'm happy when my granddad reads us a story,
and I'm happy when
I have my swimming lesson.

swimming lesson

Granddad reads us a story.

I'm happy when
I read my book,
and I'm happy when
I talk on the phone.

working

I laugh as I read my book.

I'm happy when my dad carries me on his shoulders, and I'm happy when we go to a cafe.

ordering lunch

I like riding
on my dad’s shouders.

I'm happy when
I slide on my snow tube,
and I'm happy when
I play with my dog.

playing with my dog

snow

I laugh as I slide
on my snow tube.

Home and Away Happiness

Home

Extra Vocabulary

brother

computer

shoe

snow

watch